ONE WAY OUT

The Gambler and the Credit Card Junkie

BY

Dr. Melanie Y. Duncan

©Copyright 2025 by Dr. Melanie Y. Duncan –

All rights reserved.

This book is protected by the copyright laws of the United States of America. This book may not be copied or reprinted for commercial gain or profit. Occasional page copying for group study or personal use is granted and encouraged. Unless otherwise identified, Scripture references and quotes marked KJV are taken from the King James Version of the Holy Bible.

This book is available as an eBook and paper back at most online book sellers.

All figures are royalty free Adobe Stock

Cover design photo taken by Dr. Melanie Y. Duncan

Cover designed by Dr. Melanie Y. Duncan

For Worldwide Distribution, Printed in the U.S.A.

This book is dedicated to: Jonathan and Maya,

A mother's love is forever! I adore you so much!

To Seth, I thank God for you!

I am so happy to share the rest of my life with you!

TABLE OF CONTENTS

Introduction 5

    Chapter One: Similarities 6

    Chapter Two: Understand The Devourer 11

Support System 16

Spiritual Strength 16

Boundaries 16

Action Steps 17

Affirmations 17

Fears for Moving Forward 19

    PART II: Chapter Three: Walk through the Open Door 23

    Chapter Four: How to Redeem the Time 28

Conclusion/Declaration 30

Short Prayers to Give you Hope 33

Notes and Personal Reflections 36

About the Author 37

Introduction

I congratulate you on purchasing this eBook or paperback and trust you are on a journey to make the rest of your life better! It does not matter where one begins but where one rests when the journey ends.

This short book discusses similarities between a gambler and a credit card addict and is meant to encourage and bring hope. If you have tried several ways to get it right and failed. I say to you, try again!

Do not lose heart! We all struggle with something, surround yourself with encouragement. Giving to others is one of the greatest ways to encourage yourself. If that sounds like you, I encourage you to share this book with someone who may struggle with an addiction, and those who may not have the means to purchase this eBook.

For more than 50 years, I have seen or experienced the residue of addiction. I share the one way out as a reminder that regardless of the type of addiction you may face, you can get out! Let this story encourage and empower you to keep going. I encourage you to try this one way out!

Chapter One: Similarities

Both gamblers and those in credit card debt often find themselves trapped in a cycle of risky choices, hoping for a breakthrough that rarely comes. As the stakes grow higher, the consequences multiply, leaving individuals scrambling to recover. This toxic cycle not only impacts their finances but also invades their emotional and mental well-being, leading to feelings of isolation and despair.

Many individuals caught in this cycle also face the relentless pressure of maintaining appearances, disguising their struggles from their friends and family. They often rationalize their choices, believing that one more bet or one more swipe of the card will lead to redemption. The burden they carry becomes a silent and heavy weight, eroding their capacity for joy and clarity.

Breaking free from these destructive habits often requires a monumental shift in mindset, coupled with consistent and deliberate actions. It starts with acknowledging the problem and seeking help, whether through counseling, support groups, or trusted mentors who can offer guidance and accountability. Building a foundation of self-awareness and discipline can gradually replace harmful behaviors with healthier choices.

Studies have shown that it takes 30 days to form new habits. Gambling and credit card dependency both seem to violate this theory. Gamblers and credit card dependency both seem to thrive on impulse, misplaced optimism and secrecy. It has been said that the worst thing that can happen to anyone that gambles for the first time is winning. While living in Nevada, I witnessed the expressions on the faces of those who were first time winners.

You could see the adrenaline rush on their face, and the way their body moved when someone came to take their photo. The winner not only stepped into their five minutes of fame, but they also opened the door to a new realm of instant gratification for their body, soul and mind instantaneously!

Your next fix is just around the corner. You don't have to book a trip to Nevada, you can visit your local gas station, your local laundromat, your grocery store or a liquor store to play daily lottery games, and small replicas of Las Vegas style slot machines. Over the years, I witnessed people enter and leave grocery stores without groceries, enter a laundromat with dry, dirty clothes leave with wet clean clothes or with the same dirty clothes 30 minutes after they walked in. I have heard stories of personnel being escorted until they boarded their planes to ensure they did not put anymore of the family retirement fund into a slot machine before take-off!

What about the credit cards? That is a great question! Credit cards are a gamblers' best friend! Credit cards offer easy access to cash by way of a cash advance. In the United States of America, several states do not permit the use of credit cards for purchasing lottery tickets, and lottery instant win games. The cash advance feature of credit cards allows the user to enter their credit card pin number into an ATM machine and receive cash. In other words, gambling can now resume! Never mind the 18% interest rate or higher for the cash advance, or the accumulation of unsecured credit card debt. The gambler just needs one more win and that credit card bill will go away in no time!

Euphoria! Perhaps this is the way the gambler feels once they are holding cold, hard, cash in their hands as they race back to the nearest machine, blackjack table, or high stakes poker table to win big!

I have even witnessed someone with a binder printout of all the lottery combinations for the daily pick 3 game for a particular state on the West Coast of the United States since the beginning of the daily pick 3 game! They explained that they needed the statistics on every combination to increase their chances of consistently winning the daily pick 3 game for that state. I thought to myself, what global problems could this person solve if they used this same passion toward incurable diseases or world peace?

This brings us to the traits, not passion, of gamblers based on the medical health expertise of the Mayo Clinic. According to the Mayo Clinic, compulsive gambling is referred to as a gambling disorder that stimulates the brain's reward system. Each new loss can create debt! The intertwined nature of gambling and credit card use reveals a complex landscape where hope and risk intermingle. The allure of an easy fix, whether it's one lucky hand or the swipe of a card, often masks a deeper search for relief and significance. Each attempt to escape the consequences only deepens the cycle, ensuring that <u>relief remains just out of reach</u>. There's the brief illusion of control, a moment when the next transaction or wager promises resolution, yet what follows is often remorse and renewed desperation.

But what happens when we shift our focus from gambling to credit card use? On the surface, these behaviors may seem distinct—one is associated with games of chance and the lure of jackpots, the other with everyday purchases and a sense of convenience. Yet, peel back the layers and a similar pattern emerges: a longing for control, a pursuit of relief, and the seductive promise of a quick escape from discomfort. For many, credit cards become more than a tool, they become a lifeline in moments of stress, a way to bridge the gap between desire and reality.

Compulsive credit card use is not a recognized disorder by the Mayo Clinic. Compulsive credit card use is often seen as a compulsion to shop and as a result is seen as slightly more common in women than men (https://www.addictiongroup.org/resources/shopping-addiction-statistics/). Women tend to use credit cards more strategically according to the article while men tend to use credit cards as frequently as daily, and for hobby items.

The lines between necessity and indulgence blur as swipes become reflexive rather than intentional. The monthly statements pile up; each charge a reminder of fleeting satisfaction and accumulating consequences. Unlike gambling, which carries a certain societal stigma, excessive credit card use can masquerade as normalcy, making it even harder to recognize when spending has crossed from routine to compulsive.

The psychological toll mirrors that of gambling: secrecy, guilt, and isolation. Both paths are marked by the struggle to balance hope and fear that the next purchase or payout will bring lasting change, and the fear that the cycle can never be broken. Recognizing these parallels is vital to understanding how addiction can take root in the most ordinary routines, transforming them into sources of anxiety and self-doubt.

So, we now have an idea of a few disparities that we can build from. Men are more prone to gambling addiction, frequent use of credit cards, are seen as workaholics, highly competitive and easily bored. Women are often seen as strategic shoppers based on holidays, birthdays, and special events and less likely prone to gambling addiction than men. This goes back to the questions I asked on the cover of this book, why does it seem that the nicest people struggle to find happiness? How do bad things happen to good people?

This reading aims to serve not as a mere critique of addiction but as a beacon of hope and a guide for those seeking to reclaim their lives. The content stresses the importance of perseverance and faith, reminding readers that every setback contains the seed of a comeback. For those grappling with the weight of tough choices and lingering doubts, the pages here are a call to action, an invitation to take that first bold step toward freedom.

In the next chapter, we will discuss the devourer. The circumstances, environment and choices that are trying to rob you of hope.

Chapter Two: Understand The Devourer

The devourer is not always obvious; it can manifest through subtle habits or unchecked emotions that gradually consume hope and purpose. Whether through compulsive gambling, excessive spending, or addictive behaviors, it seeks to isolate and control, feeding on moments of vulnerability and despair. Recognizing the devourer is the first step to fighting it, and understanding its tactics can arm you to reclaim your life with intentionality and strength.

Let's start with understanding the underlying triggers that drive gambling or credit card abuse. Stress, loneliness, isolation or past trauma often serve as catalysts, and addressing these root causes can be instrumental in recovery. Developing new coping mechanisms, such as engaging in fulfilling hobbies, exercising, or reconnecting with loved ones, can help fill the emotional void that these addictions often leave behind.

The journey away from addiction is rarely linear. There will be moments of doubt, setbacks, and even relapses but each day offers a new opportunity for growth. Celebrate the victories, however minor they may seem. Hold fast to the truth that progress is possible, and healing is a process, not a single event. With time, perseverance, and support, you will begin to rewrite your story—one where freedom and self-worth are reclaimed, and each day is met with hope rather than fear.

Recovery begins when we recognize that real change is not about chasing another chance, but about stepping back to see the cycle for what it is. Honesty with oneself is the first key.

Acknowledging the pattern, not as a personal failing but as a challenge that can be faced and overcome. Small steps matter!

As we peel away the layers, it becomes clear that recovery is not simply a matter of resisting temptation or curbing excess, it is a journey of rediscovery, one that calls for compassion and self-reflection. At its heart, healing from addiction demands the courage to confront pain and the willingness to replace destructive routines with moments of authentic connection and purpose.

The process begins with honest self-inquiry: What are the emotions or memories that drive you toward these patterns? What void are you trying to fill each time you reach for the cards or place a wager? By naming these triggers, you disempower them, transforming vague anxieties into tangible challenges that can be overcome.

ACTIONABLE CHANGE

Awareness alone is not enough; it must be paired with actionable change.

>Small intentional steps

>Setting spending limits

>Seeking professional guidance

>Talking openly with trusted friends—

>Help to reclaim agency and restore trust in oneself.

Recovery is not a solitary pursuit but a collective endeavor, built upon the foundations of honesty and hope. At the same time, remember that setbacks do not erase progress. Each stumble is a lesson, a chance to refine your strategy and recommit to the path ahead. The resilience you forge in these moments becomes a shield against future adversity, and the grace you extend to yourself is as vital as any external support.

Ultimately, overcoming addiction is more than breaking habits, it's about restoring a sense of possibility and worth. It's about finding joy in ordinary moments and strength in vulnerability. As you move forward, let the promise of renewal guide your steps, and trust that with each effort, you come closer to reclaiming the life you were meant to live.

Write your intentional steps, spending limits and plan for professional guidance below.

INCREMENTAL CHANGES

1. Seek support

2. Set boundaries

3. Learn to pause before acting on impulse,

These incremental changes can build the scaffolding for transformation, inch by inch.

Embracing accountability and building resilience are essential in this battle. Surround yourself with a support system that encourages transparency and growth, not judgment or condemnation.

CELEBRATE YOU. Allow yourself to celebrate every instance of progress, however modest it may seem. Consistency, not perfection, is the true measure of growth—each positive decision, each moment you choose understanding over judgment, fortifies your spirit and broadens your capacity to heal. When facing moments of doubt or fatigue, remember that change is a process. Keep moving and find new ways to celebrate you that do not require spending money. Take a walk in the park, go for a hike or visit a museum. As you continue to build your new normal and boundaries, have a plan for how to handle triggers. Remember your accountability team and speak with a trusted friend.

As you cultivate patience and self-compassion, take time to acknowledge the courage it takes to ask for help and to try again. Recovery is a mosaic of countless small victories—moments of clarity, honesty, restraint, or simple presence—that, when pieced together, reveal a life transformed.

Keeping this perspective in mind can lessen the sting of setbacks and magnify the significance of each step forward.

It's through these gentle, persistent efforts that you build a foundation for lasting recovery. Lean into the support of your community and trust in the process, even when progress feels slow. Transformation is often quiet and gradual, but each day holds the possibility of breakthrough and hope renewed.

Over the next two pages is the personal reflection and action guide. I encourage you to take time to complete this guide and use it as part of your support system.

PERSONAL REFLECTION AND ACTION GUIDE

Support System

- List the names of people or groups who offer encouragement and accountability:

- Describe the ways in which you will maintain transparency within your support system:

- Identify specific times or situations when you will reach out for help:

Spiritual Strength

- Write down spiritual truths or teachings that inspire your courage and sense of purpose:

- Describe how faith will anchor you during moments of struggle:

- List practices (prayer, meditation, fellowship) that ground and renew your spirit:

Boundaries

- List situations or triggers that challenge your recovery:

- Describe clear boundaries you will set to protect your progress:

- Write steps for enforcing these boundaries when tested:

Action Steps

- List small, intentional changes you will make in daily life to foster growth:

- Describe how you will celebrate progress without relying on spending money:

- Create a plan for addressing setbacks with patience and self-compassion:

Affirmations

- Write encouraging statements about your strength, resilience, and capacity for transformation:

- Record moments when you have overcome challenges, no matter how small.

FAITH

Faith plays a pivotal role in overcoming the devourer. Leaning on spiritual truths and drawing strength from the love of Christ can inspire courage and renew your sense of purpose. This transformation requires both grit and grace, as healing is often a process rather than a singular victory.

Through faith, fellowship, and fortitude, you can illuminate the shadows cast by the devourer. The journey may be challenging, but every small triumph builds a foundation for lasting freedom and peace. This book is here to guide you in identifying the ways addiction can sneak into your life and to equip you with the tools to confront it head-on. Remember, you are never alone in this fight, and hope remains steadfast, even in the darkest hours.

On the next page, take some time to honestly acknowledge your worries or anxieties as you embark on this journey. This page is for writing down all your fears for moving forward.

Fears for Moving Forward

- Write here any fears or concerns you feel about the changes ahead.

- Be honest—no fear is too small or too big to acknowledge.

- Remember, recognizing your fears is the first step toward overcoming them.

- Reflect on what triggers these fears and how you might gently address them.

Figure 1 Support

When we talk about the devourer it is important to remember that we are talking about life and death here. This is a fight that you must win!

Many who face addiction often feel that their struggles are a solitary battle, but it is crucial to remember that recovery is not a path meant to be walked alone. Reaching out to a community of support, one built on kindness, understanding, and accountability, can illuminate even the darkest paths.

Transparency within such relationships fosters trust and instills hope, paving the way for meaningful transformation.

Additionally, cultivating spiritual resilience can offer profound strength in the face of adversity. Faith acts as both anchor and compass, grounding an individual in love and purpose while guiding them toward renewal. The teachings of Christ, centered around forgiveness and unwavering hope, encourage a mindset of perseverance and grace that is essential for healing. Spiritual truths provide not only comfort but also a powerful framework for rebuilding one's life with dignity and courage.

This book aims to bridge the gap between understanding and action, urging readers to confront the forces that seek to consume their joy and purpose. Through intentional steps rooted in faith, fellowship, and self-awareness, the road to freedom from addiction becomes not just a possibility but a promise waiting to be fulfilled.

Each choice you make is a brick in the foundation of hope or despair. No matter the weight of past failures or the grip of current struggles, the path forward begins with acknowledging the divine strength within you and embracing it as a catalyst for change. Addiction often seeks to shackle you to a narrative of inadequacy and defeat, but breaking free requires a heart courageous enough to rewrite that story.

Remember, breaking the chains of addiction is not only a personal triumph but a spiritual awakening reclaiming of the purpose for which you were created. As you walk through these trials, let the unwavering love of Christ illuminate your steps and remind you that hope is always within reach. By leaning into faith, fostering connection, and cultivating self-awareness, you are choosing life, freedom, and restoration over the despair that addiction demands. There is an open door of redemption for you! Let's go there together in the next chapter.

- ❖ Now that we have addressed that root and the circumstances, are you ready to walk through the door of hope and restoration?

PART II: Chapter Three: Walk through the Open Door

Figure 2 The open door

In walking through the open door of healing, it is essential to embrace the concept of jubilee, a season of restoration, renewal, and release from bondage. Like the biblical jubilee, which signified the liberation of debts and the return of lost inheritances, your personal journey toward freedom can serve as a profound reclamation of your purpose and joy.

In stepping through this open door, you are invited into a season of jubilee time of restoration, renewal, and celebration. Just as the ancient jubilee signified liberty and the return of what was lost, your journey now echoes that promise. Release the burdens of yesterday and allow yourself to embrace the freedom that faith makes possible. Picture the jubilee not only as a release from bondage but as a divine invitation to reclaim joy, purpose, and connection.

As you prepare to walk through, reflect on the transformative power of surrender—to let go of old patterns and welcome the grace that God offers with open arms. This is more than a moment of relief; it is the beginning of a new chapter, where each step forward is marked by hope and possibility. The jubilee is your inheritance, a gift that calls you to celebrate the victory over addiction and to step boldly into the future that awaits.

As you cross this threshold, know that you do not walk alone. The community around you, fortified by shared faith and genuine compassion, move forward together, each person carrying a torch that lights the way for others. The jubilee is both personal and communal, extending its blessings to all who seek restoration.

Take a deep breath and step forward into the light, into the promise, into the jubilee.

Healing requires not only physical and emotional renewal, but also a spiritual awakening that acknowledges the divine truths meant to guide your steps.

As you move forward, take each day as a sacred opportunity to step into the life that God has promised. The process will not be without its trials, but every act of surrender to His grace and every intentional choice to pursue faith over fear will reshape the narrative of your life. Let gratitude be a cornerstone of this transformation, thanking God for new beginnings and for the people He has placed in your life to walk alongside you in this journey.

Jubilee is not limited to personal freedom—it extends to the impact your healing can have on others. As you share your story of redemption, you can become a beacon of hope for those still trapped in the shadows of addiction. Together, as a community bound by faith, fellowship, and resilience, you can create a ripple effect of renewal that touches lives and glorifies God's enduring love.

- ❖ Thought: In the book of Leviticus, chapter 25 (KJV), the year of jubilee occurred every 50 years. Even if you paid off your credit card in 20-30 years, you still would not reap the true benefits of full restoration from addiction!

The ongoing transformation is not simply a fleeting moment of inspiration or relief; it is the weaving of a new tapestry, thread by thread, each colored with mercy, hope, and the quiet courage to begin again. In this season, you are not merely recovering what has been taken, you are being shaped into someone new. The echoes of past bondage are gradually replaced by the grace of restored identity and rekindled dreams.

Each day brings fresh opportunities to recognize the sacredness of your journey, to nurture a heart open to gratitude, and to step forward with intention.

The journey through the open door may wind, pause, or double back. There will be moments of vulnerability, but these, too, are holy, for in your weakness, God's strength is revealed. Allow grace in the love of God to be both your anchor and your wings, holding you steady in uncertainty and lifting you into new vistas of possibility. Healing in the jubilee is not about erasing the past but allowing its lessons to give depth and meaning to the present.

As you continue forward, honor God and give Him thanks for your progress. No step is too small, no victory too quiet to celebrate God. In this way, your personal jubilee ripples out reflecting the love of God and calling others to courage, healing, and hope.

Every step of healing, every prayer whispered in moments of despair, and every act of surrender to the transformative power of faith builds a foundation not only for personal renewal but for the community around you. Healing is a journey that bridges past wounds and future promises, uniting them in the present through the grace of God. It is a testament to the truth that no matter how deep the valley, the peaks of redemption and hope await.

Let this journey inspire others, reminding them that they, too, can break free from the chains that seek to confine their spirit. By walking in faith and leaning on the love of Christ, you are declaring that hope is stronger than despair, and freedom is near for anyone willing to step into the open door of redemption in Christ.

❖ Can you redeem the 20-30 years or more of your life that were stolen in the battle? Let's discuss this answer in the next chapter!

The path through jubilee reminds us that faith is not meant to be static but a dynamic force that propels us forward. As you embrace this season, consider the profound invitation to not only restore what has been lost but to reimagine what is possible. The grace of God is abundant, overflowing, and always sufficient to fill the voids left by addiction and fear.

Chapter Four: How to Redeem the Time

In chapter three we began a discussion on redeeming the time. In this final chapter we discuss the path for redeeming the time. Redeeming the time starts with a promise. The promise is not based on how much you won or loss, your age, your sex, your sexual orientation, race, color or creed.

YOU cannot redeem your time!

True redemption requires an unwavering commitment to God's promises and a willingness to trust His divine plan. It begins with the recognition that time lost to addiction and despair cannot be reclaimed through human effort alone. Instead, we are called to surrender our burdens to Christ—a surrender that paves the way for renewal, restoration, and transformation. By embracing the truth of Joel 2:25 (KJV), we acknowledge that God's power to restore extends beyond the tangible, reaching into the deepest recesses of our hearts and minds. Redemption becomes the bridge between the pain of the past and the hope of the future, a pathway illuminated by His love and grace.

- ❖ The Lord, the maker of heaven and earth! Jehovah Jireh, (the Lord who provides), **He can redeem the time for you**! The Lord promises to restore the years the locust (destroyer of your crops), the cankerworm (destroyer down to the root), the caterpillar (toxins) and the Palmer worm (eats the fruit of the increase) stole!

Through faith, you are invited to witness the unfolding of divine restoration, a process that transcends physical belongings and ventures into the realms of emotional and spiritual recovery.

The act of redeeming lost time is not limited to regaining the years overshadowed by hardship; it also encompasses the cultivation of new moments filled with grace, purpose, and joy. It is a reaffirmation that every single day ahead can be infused with the richness of God's blessings.

As Malachi 3:10-11 reminds us, the act of giving—of entrusting your resources to God—becomes a deeply spiritual gesture through which an abundance of blessings is unlocked. Redemption is echoed not only in the restoration of what was stolen but in the multiplication of opportunities to glorify His name. In essence, what is given in faith is returned manifold, not only in material gain but in spiritual fulfillment and peace.

Take heart knowing that this path of renewal is paved with promises that are not bound by earthly limitations. By surrendering to Christ and honoring His word, you declare to the world that your faith is steadfast, your hope unwavering, and your spirit unbroken. The process of redeeming time becomes a testament to the enduring power of the Gospel, marking every step forward with the light of His love and the assurance that His grace is sufficient for all.

- ❖ Have you been promised this kind of rate of return from gambling or from credit card companies?

Conclusion/Declaration

Over the last 4 chapters we discussed addiction, hope and redeeming the time. We discussed your bright future and promises. There is just one more step to unlock the key to certainty!

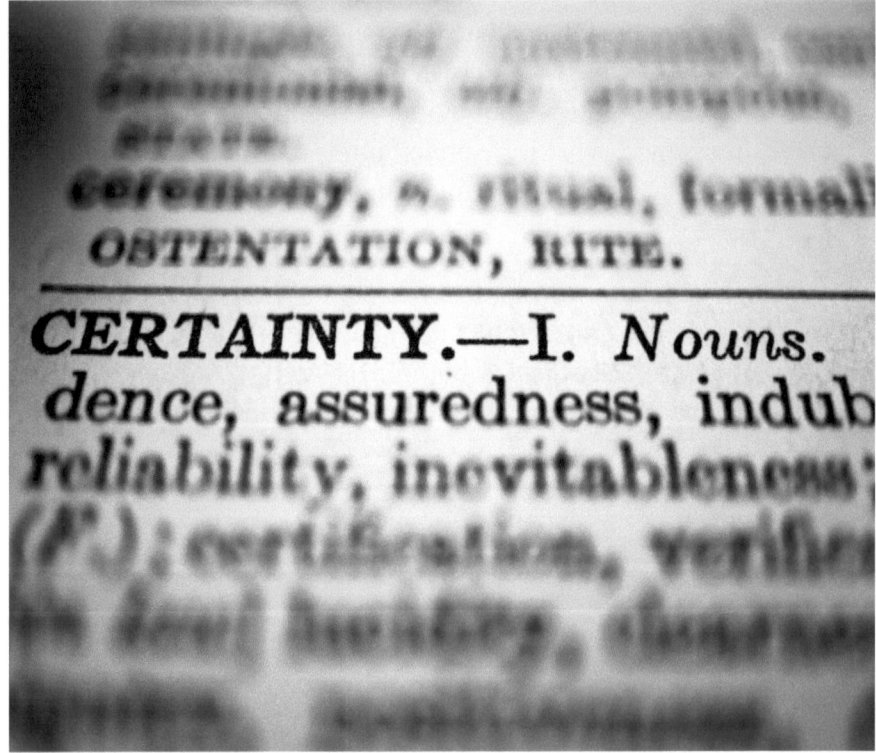

Figure 3 Certainty

As you stand at this crossroads, reflect on the magnitude of God's promises and the life-changing impact of unwavering faith. The essence of redemption is not solely about reclaiming what was lost, but about stepping into a new realm of possibilities, where grace and love guide each step forward.

It is a transformative journey, where the scars of the past tell a story of resilience, and the hope for the future shines brightly.

Embrace the invitation to turn your eyes upon Jesus, the author and finisher of faith. It is through Him that your burdens are lifted, your heart is restored, and your spirit finds peace.

Action	Result
Shift from putting your money in a man's pot of robbery to Kingdom purpose	God can move on your behalf; God can move on behalf of your situation and restore you to His full intent before there was an earth

<u>You have hope!</u>
<u>You are not hopeless</u>!
<u>You are not defeated!</u>

Pray with me,

Lord Jesus, I repent for seeking things to fill the void in my life that only you can fill. I have a God-shaped hole! I have tried to fill it with temporary pleasures, and it has not worked for my good. Your Word says you would work **all things** together for good for those who love the Lord and are called according to his purpose (Romans 8:28, KJV).

Father today, I choose you! I choose to follow Christ! Jesus take my life! Take my sin! Take my addictions! I repent, and I ask you to come into my heart. I ask you to fill my God-shaped hole with you. Fill all my empty voids with you. Fill me with your love and with your power. I ask you to be:

Lord of my life	**Lord of my purpose**
Lord of my destiny	**Lord of my will**

I want to live for you Jesus. I accept your free gift and invite you to come into my heart and be my Lord. I ask you to be my Savior. I ask you to be my deliverer. I ask you to be my peace. I ask you to make me all that I was destined to be for you. I want to live for you!

I love you Lord and it is in the name of Jesus that I petition this prayer and declaration to you!

Thank you, Abba (Father), for welcoming me home with your ring, your robe, a seat at your table and for establishing me and making me the righteousness of God in Christ (2 Corinthians 5:21).

Short Prayers to Give you Hope

I have written a two short prayers and a petition you can use for daily meditation on God's Word.

PRAYER #1

Abba (Father) I ask you for Chokmah (wisdom), the ability to make right and wise choices at the opportune time.

I want to develop in maturity and special ability given by you alone in accordance with Exodus 35.31.

Fill me with the Spirit of God is wisdom, in understanding, and in knowledge and in all manner of workmanship.

I realize from your word that to receive this from you I must have a holy fear and reverence of you.

May I bind mercy and truth to my neck and write them on the table of my heart. May I find favor with you and man as I do these things.

PRAYER #2

Lord create in me a true desire to follow you and experience true intimacy that can only be found in you.

Remove pride and self-reliance from my heart that I may truly experience the mind of Christ (1 Corinthians 2:16).

Your wisdom is pure, peaceable, gentle and easy to pursue. You are full of mercy and good fruits (Galatians 5:22-25) like joy, peace, goodness, gentleness, faith, temperance, meekness and long-suffering. Teach me to make peace so the fruit of righteousness is sewn in me (James 3:17-18).

Lord your understanding is perfect. I am made perfect in my weakness.

Grant me the Spirit of wise counsel to know where the enemy is lurking against me.

WHAT DO I WANT FROM GOD? PROMISES OF ISAIAH 11:1-2

Lord I want to walk in my royal family line of King David.
I want the Spirit of Yahweh to rest on me
I want the Spirit of extraordinary wisdom
I want the Spirit of perfect understanding
I want the Spirit of wise strategy
I want the Spirit of mighty power
I want the Spirit of Revelation
I want the Spirit of the fear of Yahweh
I want the delight of living in the 7 dimensions of the Holy Spirit
I want the illuminating influence of God over me
I want the warrior sash of righteousness and belt of faithfulness
You the creator of the universe have numbered every hair on my head
You the creator of the universe cares about me by name
You see me as the perfection you made me to be
I am called to be the righteousness of God in Christ (2 Corinthians 5:21)
I am called out of darkness into your marvelous light
I am redeemed from the law
I am redeemed from the curse
I am redeemed from fear of man

<u>Jesus, the One Way Out!</u>

Notes and Personal Reflections

- What insights or thoughts came to your mind as you reflected on these truths?

- How have you experienced redemption in your own life?

- Are there specific fears or burdens you feel called to lay down today?

- List moments when you sensed God's care and love for you personally.

- Write a prayer, affirmation, or verse to anchor your faith this week.

About the Author

Dr. Melanie Y. Duncan is a Navy Veteran and retired Civil Servant. For more than 40 years she has seen or experienced the residue of addiction. Dr. Duncan shares the one way out as a reminder that regardless of the type of addiction you may face, you can get out! Let this book encourage and empower you to keep going! You are encouraged to try this one way out! Share your results with friends and family and use this book and your story to empower others!

Dr. Duncan has been a Christian since 1979 and enjoys sharing the love of Christ, that all may experience this amazing love!

www.ingramcontent.com/pod-product-compliance
Lightning Source LLC
Chambersburg PA
CBHW041822040426
42453CB00005B/133